DICKENS IN RO

CW00433028

His books and the festivals

Charles Dickens in 1852.
Photo: Dickens House Museum, London.

Shirley Harrison and Sally Evemy

S.B. Publications

First published in 1997 by S. B. Publications,
c/o 19 Grove Road, Seaford, East Sussex BN25 1TP

ISBN 1 85770 126 7

Designed and typeset by CGB Lewes
Printed by Island Press Ltd
3 Cradle Hill Industrial Estate, Seaford, East Sussex BN25 3JE
Tel: 01323 490222

CONTENTS

ABOUT THE AUTHORS

SHIRLEY HARRISON and Sally Evemy joined forces as The Word Team in 1992. Shirley has been a national journalist and author for more than forty years and her books include the *Welcome* travel guides for Collins 1980/2/3; *New Approaches to Cancer*, Century 1987; and *The Channel – dividing link*, Collins 1986.

Sally researches and edits.

Together they have worked on *Cults, the Battle for God* and *The Diary of Jack the Ripper* which is an international best seller. They have also scripted *The White Cliffs Experience* at Dover, the *Living Legend* on Jersey, the Oxford Story and the Mappa Mundi Exhibition at Hereford Cathedral. In 1995 they published *Rochester Upon Medway, the Tale of a City*.

ACKNOWLEDGEMENTS

MANY people have helped us in the preparation of this book.

In particular we would like to thank Thelma Grove, who shared her expert knowledge of Dickens with us and checked the text; Bob Ratcliffe of the City of Rochester Society; Huw Jarvis and the hard working team at the Civic Centre; Dr David Parker and the staff at the Dickens House Museum; Mrs Marguerite Taylor for her help with illustrations and the staff at the Local Studies Centre, Rochester Upon Medway.

PICTURE CREDITS

Pictures of Charles Dickens and members of his family are reproduced by courtesy of the Dickens House Museum, London and are individually credited. Other pictures have been kindly supplied by Rochester Upon Medway City Council, the Guildhall Museum, Rochester, the Medway News, R L Ratcliffe and the Fine Art Studios, Strood and are also individually credited.

Front cover: Some famous Dickens' characters in their festival finery. Photo: Medway News

Back cover: A Dickensian Christmas scene of skaters on a flooded and frozen street. Photo: Rochester Upon Medway City Council.

FOREWORD

IN view of the close association of Charles Dickens with Rochester, some visitors are surprised there is no Dickens statue or monument, apart from the memorial tablet in the Cathedral.

In Dickens's will, he directed that he should not be made 'the subject of any monument, memorial or testimonial whatever. I rest my claims to the remembrance of my country upon my published works.'

The annual Rochester Dickens Festivals and Dickensian Christmases described in this book convincingly demonstrate that remembrance of Charles Dickens, his writings and the host of characters peopling them are celebrated by thousands of residents and visitors in 'the birthplace of his fancy'.

Local people say: 'It always rains for Dickens,' and over the eighteen years there certainly have been some rained-on parades and damp costumes. Those of us wearing several heavy skirts, tight fitting bodices, long sleeves and gloves, remember many very hot days when we looked enviously at visitors in T shirts and sun-tops. Snow is guaranteed at the Dickensian Christmas from the snow-machines, although their first appearance prompted genuine falls of snow.

Shirley and Sally have captured the joy and enthusiasm Dickens inspires, and if the reader has not already visited the Festival, this book will persuade him or her to remedy the omission.

Thelma Grove
Chairman, Dickens Fellowship Rochester.

FESTIVAL CELEBRITIES

BILL SIKES, housebreaker and thief in *Oliver Twist*. Left are two characters from *Great Expectations*, ABEL MAGWITCH, Pip's convict benefactor and the eccentric recluse, Miss Havisham, in her wedding dress. *Photos: Rochester Upon Medway City Council.*

1

WHY ROCHESTER?

THE Dickens Festival celebrates, above all else, the special place of Rochester and its surrounding countryside in Charles Dickens' books and in his heart.

It was Dickens' unique talent, humour and eye for detail that focused the attention of the world on the City of Rochester upon Medway and established its place in literature. Even in his lifetime the people of Rochester were proud of the celebrity he brought their historic city. He spent five idyllic childhood years here from 1817 to 1822. He was a national legend when he returned for the last thirteen years of his life, dying at Gad's Hill in 1870.

Because his books were originally serialised, in weekly and monthly magazines, they reached a huge public in much the same way as do soap operas today. His characters, many of whom originated in the area, were loved in every home.

But Dickens wrote with an eye on posterity. He was always confident that his books would be placed amongst the greats.

It is less well known that throughout his life Dickens was also passionate about the theatre. 'Do you know what would be the realisation of my most wonderful day dream? To sit down for the remainder of my days near a theatre where I would hold supreme authority. That is my day dream.'

For Dickens was so much more than one of the world's greatest novelists. He was also an entertainer, a natural star, an exhibitionist followed by fans, autographing wine bottles, long before stars were born.

With his bushy beard, flashy weskits, his overlong loose check trousers, necktie awry and carrying his small dog whip, he took daily walks, always at a great pace, usually down the middle of the road. The Rochester post-

A mural in the Civic Centre, Strood shows aspects of Dickensian Rochester and the great writer at his desk in his study at Gad's Hill.
Photo: Rochester Upon Medway City Council

man once recalled how he could be seen acting to himself as he walked, his face constantly in motion.

He was greedy for life, craved publicity and would have revelled in the razzmatazz that has inevitably crept into his Festival.

Gerald Dickens, who enthusiastically travels the country with one-man dramatisations of his great great grandfather's works, believes that had Dickens been alive today he would probably have been an international impresario – at the heart of it all, making things happen.

He would have been out there, promoting, organising, acting and soaking up the public acclaim of his books and the affectionate annual re-creation of his characters by the people of Rochester around the time of the late spring bank holiday. The monster blow-up fairground hammers, the candyfloss and enthusiastic crowds – he would have loved it all. He was a showman through and through and Rochester's Festival is his show.

2

CHARLES AS A CHILD

CHARLES DICKENS was born in Portsmouth on 7 February 1812, the second child of John Dickens, a naval pay clerk, and his wife, Elizabeth.

When Charles' parents moved to Chatham in 1817, the town had the reputation of being the wickedest place in the world. Into its already over-crowded, dirty streets had been thrown the flotsam and jetsam from the recently ended Napoleonic wars. Sailors with peg legs, maimed soldiers, all with nowhere to go and nothing to do frequented the numerous ale houses and brothels. Chained convicts from the hulks staggered to and fro, while through the dank, Medway–borne mist moved the masts of the victorious British fleet and across the fields echoed the clanging and banging of the dockyard at work. Up river, by contrast, was the cloistered world of old Rochester with its ancient High Street, its castle and its cathedral watching over all.

Three children – soon there would be five – and two nurses, Mary Weller and Jane Bonny, moved with John and Elizabeth Dickens and her sister Mary, known as Aunt Fanny, into the little house in Ordnance Terrace. It had been recently built, on the brow of the hill, pleasantly above the bustle of Chatham and overlooking corn fields. It was here that Charles Dickens said he 'beat violently against the gates of the world.'

Even as a small boy, Charles was spellbound by all things theatrical. He told his lifelong friend and biographer, John Forster, how he would be 'elevated on chairs and tables' to sing small comic songs to the family. As an adult 'he blushed to think what a horrible little nuisance he must have been to so many unoffending grown up people who were called upon to admire him.'

Charles' father, John, who had such an influence on his son's development, was a good-looking, cheery but utterly improvident clerk in the Chatham Navy Pay Office. He once described himself as 'a cork which, when submerged, bobs up to the surface again none the worse for the dip'.

John's father-in-law, too, had a way with money. He was employed in the Navy Pay office in London in the very senior rank of Chief Conductor of Moneys in Town. But in seven years he mulcted the Navy Board of more than £5,000 and, when discovered, confessed and fled the country.

Fortunately Charles did not inherit the family improvidence. As he became successful he was increasingly irritated by the inability of his parents, his siblings and his own children to manage their affairs and their constant reliance on his generosity.

'All of them,' he wrote many years later, 'look upon me as something to be pluckéd and torn to pieces for their advantage.'

Friends claimed that it was from Dickens' mother, an intelligent, boisterous, somewhat disorganised woman, that Charles inherited his talent for mimicry and sharp eye for detail. She taught him his lessons every day, including Latin, and instilled in him a love of words. 'I dreamed my first dreams of authorship when I was six years old or so,' he once said.

His first recorded work from this time is a short story, *Misnar, Sultan of India*, probably inspired by his favourite *Arabian Nights*.

Mary Weller read bedtime stories to Charles, scaring him with what he called 'nightmares and perspirations'. Much later he recalled the first books that he read alone, discovered in the attic, with their 'deliciously smooth covers of red and green.'

He fell in love for the first time, he claimed, with Little Red Riding Hood. In real life his seven year old heart was given to the girl next door. Her name was Lucy Stroughill, 'a peach faced creature in a blue sash.'

Life was convivial and the little house on the hill was the centre of much entertaining. There were birthday parties and Christmas, New Year and Twelfth Night parties during which the children performed. There was community singing and lots of games and magic lantern shows.

Charles had also been known to stand on a table at gatherings in the Mitre Inn in Chatham (long since disappeared beneath British Home Stores in Chatham High Street). There he sang duets with his elder sister

Fanny. His favourite recitation performed, according to Mary Weller, with 'such attitudes', was *The Voice of the Sluggard*.

Warmest among his memories were those of sitting on the hard, narrow seats of the Theatre Royal in Rochester, 'a sweet, dingy, shabby little country theatre'. The pictures which were stored then in his imagination appear time and time again in his stories – the smell of orange peel and sweat, lamp oil and sawdust, the sound of clapping, laughter and the tears. He sat in that 'dear. . . uncomfortable. . .flea-haunted. . .' theatre, entranced.

According to Peter Ackroyd's biography, 'he loved the bad acting and the stage costumes, the absurdity of the actors and the banality of the plays.' It was amid such scenes that the imagination of the young Dickens struggled to be born.

But above all, he loved the 'jocund world' of pantomime. He was on occasions taken to London where, in 1820, he clapped his hands 'with great precocity' at the performance of the celebrated clown Grimaldi. Years later Dickens was to edit the memoirs of the high spirited Grimaldi, whose character so closely resembled his own. 'Idleness wearied him more than labour. . .'

All his life Dickens admired the world of the clown in which all problems dissolve into laughter. He also sat, transfixed, at performances given during the travelling fairs in Rochester. Pantaloon and Columbine were his heroes, in a violent, coarse, tragi-comic world full of patriotic songs and romantic verse. Their well worn story, repeated year after year, was that of the old man marrying his daughter to a wealthy suitor although she loves another. It was followed by the Harlequinade with its slapstick and mime so clearly described by young Pip in *Great Expectations*.

The early closeness of mother and son was eventually disrupted when Charles was sent to a Dame School, above a dyer's shop in Rome Lane, Chatham.

In 1821 it was necessary to tighten the family purse strings and they moved to a more economic house in St Mary's, the Brook, next to the Baptist Meeting House. Charles also changed to a school in Clover Lane. It was run by William Giles, a young Baptist minister, for whom he retained affectionate memories.

There were thrilling days spent with his father, down at Chatham Docks; long walks together over the fields and down by the river front.

One of their favourite excursions was out to the countryside beyond Strood, where the little boy was first captivated by Gad's Hill. His father told him then: 'If you were to be very persevering and to work hard, you might some day come to live in it.'

In 1822 the unthinkable happened. Heavily in debt, John Dickens was moved to London. Charles was ten years old and forcibly uprooted from his childhood. To add to the misery, his favourite nurse, Mary Weller, married and left them. His world was crumbling.

Charles is believed to have stayed behind for about three months but then was packed off, the only passenger in the coach from Rochester. He joined his parents, brothers and sisters and a workhouse orphan, who had been adopted as a servant to replace Mary, in a tiny house in then rural Camden Town. Years later he recalled the cruel pain of that journey:

'Through all the years that have since passed have I ever lost the smell of the damp straw in which I was packed – like game – and forwarded, carriage paid, to the Cross Keys, Wood Street, Cheapside, London? . . . I consumed my sandwiches in solitude and dreariness, and it rained hard all the way, and I thought life sloppier than I had expected to find it.'

THE YEARS BETWEEN

DICKENS spent the rest of his life struggling to recapture the memory of the childhood dream he felt he had lost.

The bewildered and unhappy boy took to wandering through the back streets and alleys of Camden, the City and especially Limehouse, with its familiar riverside sights and sounds and smells. Further and further he explored . . . down to the City and to Covent Garden, a child bemused and in a dream. He was chased by vagabonds, went to the theatre alone and fed himself from the cooked food stalls. He was lonely but happier than staying at home with nothing to do, in a house hounded by creditors.

Dickens' memory of this period was coloured by his over active imagination. He lay, miserably, in his garret dreaming of Chatham and Rochester, cheated of his hopes for fame and fortune.

To add insult to injury, John Dickens decided to spend what little money he had boarding Charles' talented sister Fanny at the Royal College of Music. Charles, who loved her dearly, so badly yearned for schooling himself. He felt betrayed, 'stabbed'.

Finances did not improve and so they all moved again, this time to a house in Gower Street North. It was here that Mrs Dickens opened her Establishment for Young Ladies in an attempt to raise funds. But no pupils came.

In 1824 Charles' father was committed to the Marshalsea Prison in Southwark for debt and Mrs Dickens and the youngest children went too.

Two days after his birthday, twelve year old Charles started a job in a blacking factory, beneath Hungerford Bridge. On February 9 1824 he trudged the three miles from his lodgings to work – and three miles back again – for the first time. He was angry and bitter about his lost education, as though life itself had been cut short.

His thirteen months at the blacking factory left an indelible mark. A sensitive, bookish boy with a posh accent, his childish imagination fed upon the experience and it became a monster in his mind. He suffered untold misery, walking after work across the river, sometimes with Fanny, into the sordid squalor of Southwark and the violent rabble congregating around the Marshalsea. These experiences he described time and again – in *Oliver Twist*, *Little Dorrit* and *David Copperfield*. The damp, the rats and the stench haunted him all his life.

John Dickens was released after fourteen weeks, as a result of something Micawber-like 'turning up'. His mother-in-law had died and left them a little money, but he was dismissed from his job and from then on the family moved constantly, over-spending and incurring more and more debt.

Despite this John over-ruled Elizabeth and in 1825 Charles went back to school for two years, attending Wellington House Academy in Hampstead Road. He was an exuberant, mischievous and intelligent pupil but never forgave his mother for her opposition to his continuing education.

Family finances were no better by 1827 when another baby, Augustus, was born. Money ran out. Charles' schooling came to an end.

Elizabeth Dickens used her family connections to find Charles a job and he joined the staff of lawyers, Ellis and Blackmore, in Grays Inn. At the age of fifteen Charles Dickens 'began the world'.

Dickens the Actor – as Sir Charles Coldstream in an amateur production of *Used Up*, **from an oil painting by Augustus Egg.** *Photo: Dickens House Museum, London.*

3

BEGINNING THE WORLD

TO lighten the somewhat tedious work he rekindled his childhood love of acting. He went to the theatre every night and often put on plays in the kitchen of a neighbour's house, writing and performing dramas of every kind. He could mimic the popular singers of the day, recite pages of Shakespeare, sing and even dance.

But the job still bored him and within eighteen months he had learned shorthand and set up as a freelance correspondent in Doctors Commons, hoping to report law suits.

There, in 1830, he fell passionately in love for the first time. The lady, with the reputation of being a tantalising flirt, was pretty, vivacious, Maria Beadnell.

Dickens later wrote of her as Dora Spenlow in *David Copperfield*: 'I was swallowed up in an abyss of love in an instant.'

In 1832, when he was twenty years old, perhaps to make himself more interesting, more of a catch to Maria, he wrote to the stage manager of Covent Garden. 'I have', he said, 'a natural power of reproducing in my own person what I observe in others.' He was called for an audition and arranged to be accompanied on the piano by his sister, Fanny.

But he was 'laid up with a terrible bad cold and inflammation of the face.' The audition was cancelled and he never tried professional acting again. However, all his life he was involved with amateur theatricals. He spoke of 'creating a book in company.'

'I was born to be the manager of a theatre', he once said. He eventually formed an amateur company and over the years it produced a variety of entertainment – drama, comedy, music hall – all performed to a willing audience of invited family and friends.

He drove himself hard and expected others to do the same, insisting that his cast was punctual, thoroughly rehearsed and word perfect. He had to be in control. 'If you could see me with my coat off, the stage manager and universal director, urging impractical ladies and impossible gentlemen on to the very confines of insanity,' he wrote.

His energy was formidable. Costumes, carpentry, acting, directing, writing, he did it all. He was also extremely vain. There is a story that he refused an audience with Queen Victoria after a private performance in London because he would not allow himself to be seen by Royalty in his clown's dressing gown, absurd wig, red shiny nose and 'farce dress'. Paradoxically, it was rumoured that Queen Victoria offered Dickens a peerage and that he declined, preferring to remain plain Charles Dickens.

Dickens pursued Maria Beadnell for three years, with very little success, until in May 1833 he gave up: 'Destitute as I am of hope or comfort I have borne much and dare say I can bear more.'

Perhaps to take his mind off his broken heart, this was the year that Dickens began writing in earnest.

DICKENS THE WRITER

HIS first article, *A Dinner at Poplar Walk,* appeared in the *Monthly Magazine* in December 1833. He was not paid, but the editor asked for more. In 1836 Dickens used the pseudonym Boz for the first time. It was derived from Moses, the family nickname for his young brother Augustus. He had, by then, also become a parliamentary reporter and was contributing regularly to a number of magazines and newspapers.

In February 1836, *Sketches by Boz* appeared and a month later the first instalment of his first major novel, *The Posthumous Papers of the Pickwick Club* was published. In 1837, a new magazine was launched; edited by Dickens. It was called *Bentley's Miscellany* and included three satirical essays about Mudfog (Chatham).

The first of these Mudfog Papers, *The Public Life of Mr Tulrumble,* deals with the electoral cavortings of the pompous mayor, Nicholas Tulrumble. The second, a satire on scientists, sociologists and statisticians concerns a 'Full report of the First Meeting of The Mudfog Association for the

Advancement of Everything.' A report of the Second Meeting followed in 1838, nearly a year later.

Charles Dickens was a professional sponge with the journalist's insatiable appetite for life. According to fellow writer, Leigh Hunt, 'he had the life and soul of fifty human beings.'

His energy drove him to expose the appalling conditions of the poor in Victorian England and to campaign for the under-privileged throughout his life. Prostitutes, slaves, workhouse and ragged school children, refuse collectors – he fought for them all.

At the same time, the serious message was offset and heightened by Dickens' effervescent humour, shrewd eye for detail and witty way with words. Nothing escaped him. The larger than life characters he created come from all classes. People today who have never read Dickens' books have seen film adaptations or musicals and can relate to Mr Pickwick, Sarah Gamp, Oliver Twist, the Artful Dodger and Peggotty.

Over the next thirty seven years he worked in overdrive, every day walking for as long as he wrote – innumerable essays, letters, plays, short stories and fifteen major novels.

Many of his characters were, according to Dickens himself, drawn in one way or another from his observations of the people and places in and around what is now the City of Rochester upon Medway.

Dickens' relations with his publishers were often stormy, for despite the popularity of his writing he often earned much less than he felt due to him. Only later, when he embarked on a punishing routine of public readings, was financial success ensured.

A FAMILY MAN

IN 1834 'dearest Mouse' had come into his life. Catherine Hogarth was as quiet and moody as Maria Beadnell had been vivacious and she was overshadowed by the boisterous genius of her husband-to-be. But they were married in 1836.

The following year their first son, Charley, was born and the extraordinary success of *Pickwick* put Dickens in a position to lease his first real London home, 48 Doughty Street, and to employ a servant.

Within a month of moving to Doughty Street, Catherine's seventeen year old sister, Mary, who lived with the couple, died unexpectedly. Her death was a shock from which Dickens never fully recovered. He kept all her clothes, put her ring on his finger and treasured a lock of her hair. He even talked of being buried in her grave. 'Thank God,' he wrote, 'the very last words she whispered were of me.'

His grief was to be eased – although later complicated – when, in 1842, Mary and Catherine's younger sister, Georgina, moved in to help with the children. Georgina never married and devoted her life to her brother-in-law and his family.

The family never seemed to put foot to ground. Like his father before him, Dickens was always on the move – but, unlike his father, his rapidly improving financial situation enabled him to travel in some style and to rent comfortable villas in beautiful surroundings all over Europe. He entertained lavishly too.

The couple were to produce ten children – Charley, born 1837, Mary known as Mamie in 1838, Kate in 1839, Walter in 1840, Francis in 1843, Alfred in 1845, Sydney in 1847, Henry in 1849, Dora in 1850 and Edward in 1852. It was an amazing achievement, especially as Catherine endured difficult pregnancies and was subject to post-natal depressions.

The marriage seemed happy and affectionate in the early years. When the children were young Dickens was a wonderful father, full of fun and games, adored by them all and later by his eldest son Charley's first six children who called him 'Venerables'.

By 1839 the family was growing fast and so they moved to Devonshire Terrace off Marylebone Road.

In 1842, Dickens and a reluctant Catherine, who suffered from sea sickness, left Liverpool aboard the *Britannia* for America. By this time, as the author of *Pickwick, Oliver Twist, Nicholas Nickleby, The Old Curiosity Shop* and *Barnaby Rudge*, he was given a hero's welcome and feted wherever he went.

But there was no copyright arrangement in America and, despite his celebrity, the financial rewards from his books were nil. Even for the publicity-loving Dickens, the American press proved too much. 'I don't like the country' he wrote home, 'I would not live here on any consideration.'

Undaunted by his experience of 'abroad' Dickens took the entire family, their servants and a dog off to Italy in 1844. He had learned Italian

Two days after his birthday in February 1858, he gave one of his most powerful addresses on behalf of the hospital, in which he described a visit to the slums of Edinburgh.

'Our way went from one to another of the most wretched dwellings – reeking with horrible odours – shut off from the sky – shut out from the air – mere pits and dens. In a room in one of these places, where there was an empty porridge pot on the cold hearth, with a ragged woman and some ragged children crouching on the bare ground near it – where, I remember as I speak, that the very light, reflected from a high damp-stained house wall, came trembling in, as if the fever which had shaken everything else there had shaken even it – there lay, in an old egg box which the mother had begged from the shop, a little feeble, wasted, wan sick child.'

Years later, Dr Charles West, founder of the hospital said: 'Charles Dickens, the children's friend . . . like the good fairy in the tale gave her the gift that she should win love and favour everywhere: and so she grew and prospered.'

PARTING

INCREASINGLY, he found Catherine slow and incompetent but he was also ailing himself. Not surprisingly, with advancing years and so many children, Catherine appeared to lose her energy and Dickens complained often of her lassitude and 'mental disorder.'

At the start of 1858 Catherine Dickens had become aware of the existence of Ellen Ternan and her place in Charles' heart and by May Dickens finally separated from his wife. It was a tortuous parting.

It is from their daughter Kate, speaking of her mother, that we see a very different picture of this long-suffering and sad woman from that painted by Dickens himself.

'There was nothing wrong with my mother; she had her faults, of course, as we all have – but she was a sweet, kind, peace-loving woman, a lady – a lady born . . . My father was like a madman when my mother left home. . . this affair brought out all that was worst and all that was weakest in him. He did not care a damn what happened to any of us. Nothing could surpass the misery and unhappiness of our house.'

Dickens had also become more and more critical and remote from his growing children.

Charley said: 'He lived, I am sure two lives, one with us and one with his fictitious people and I am equally certain that the children of his brain were much more real to him at times than we were.'

Charley went to live with his mother, the other boys were at schools abroad. Only Edward remained at Gad's Hill with Mamie, Kate and the devoted Aunt Georgie, Catherine's sister. She elected to remain in order, she said, to look after the little boy and his father. She did not see her sister until Catherine was dying twenty years later.

The anguished Catherine never forgot Dickens. Sometimes she went to see his plays, tears running down her face. She kept his letters as proof of the love she felt he once had for her and photographs of the famous people she had met with him.

Kate recalled the nightmare of it all, years afterwards: 'we were all very wicked not to take her part . . . My father was not a gentleman . . . did not understand women . . . he was not a good man, he was not a fast man, but he was wonderful.'

Family life did not improve. In addition to his broken marriage, his favourite, Kate, defied her father and married. His brother, Alfred, also died. The following year, 1861, Charley too married against his father's wishes.

Dickens took his personal letters into the garden at Gad's Hill and burned them and at Christmas, in sub-zero temperatures, all the water pipes froze; almost symbolically, the house became too cold for the remaining family to sit down for their traditional Christmas dinner.

The breakdown of his marriage he bore with resignation talking of 'dismal failure'. Yet he continued to be dramatically and emotionally distracted by the idea of 'the wild energy' of true love. As a young man, he had even declared himself to be in love with Queen Victoria: 'My heart is in Windsor' he had written.

He loved the thought of being in love yet was quite incapable of finding his ideal partner. None of the female characters in his books have real depth or find true happiness.

5

ALONE AT GAD'S HILL

GAD'S HILL is a Queen Anne house, 'old fashioned, plain and comfortable', was how Dickens described it. From the roof he could see his two worlds of London and the Medway valley. But Dickens was not really a countryman at heart.

He planted the garden with his favourite bright red geraniums but the silence disturbed him and at first he would get up in the middle of the night and patrol the grounds with a gun.

His answer to the peace and quiet was to fill the house with family and with guests. Many of the best known names of the day made their way down to Rochester. Dickens exhausted everyone with vigorous long walks, sports, games, evening dramatisations of his books and renderings of his favourite parlour songs.

One of his favourite guises was that of the magician and conjuror. Dressed extravagantly, and equipped with what appeared to be the entire magic stock of Hamley's toy shop, he would transform a box of bran into a guinea pig, find a pudding in a empty saucepan and make coins fly through the air. He called himself The Unparalleled Necromancer Rhia Rhama Rhoos whose tricks included The Travelling Doll Wonder and The Conflagration Wonder..

During these last years of his life, his six grandchildren loved 'Venerables' to play the clown, flopping about like a rag doll; one day he tumbled, by accident, and to their delight fell into a bath of water. Dickens derived lifelong pleasure from all such shared entertainment. His staff at Gad's Hill remembered him rehearsing his characters in front of a long mirror, gesticulating and posing, talking to himself.

In 1860 the remarkable, soul-searching narrative of *Great Expectations* was published, together with the start of a series of autobiographical and retrospective essays, *The Uncommercial Traveller*. Several of these again focused on Rochester and its surrounding countryside.

In 1863 Charles Dickens' mother died, senile and unlamented.

The same year Dickens decided to sell the lease of Tavistock House, although he still rented another house in Peckham, where Ellen Ternan joined him from time to time. Before long she had also become a visitor to Gad's Hill, where even Georgina welcomed her warmly.

In 1863 it appears that Ellen Ternan and her mother became paying guests of the Chateau of Beaucourt Mutuel near Boulogne, where, it is claimed, Charles Dickens visited them regularly in secret. Understandably, the young actress was flattered by the attention of this famous man, although there seems to be no proof that they were lovers. Once again Charles felt bereft of 'the one thing missing in his life.'

A regular visitor to Gad's Hill, for whom Dickens developed a strange attachment, was French actor and, according to some, 'a wastrel', Charles Fechter. Wastrel or no, in 1864 Dickens took delivery of fifty six packing cases which had arrived at Higham station. They contained a full-size Swiss chalet in ninety four pieces – a Christmas gift from Mr Fechter – to be erected in the garden of Gad's Hill.

The two-roomed chalet became Dickens' hideaway, his secret place among the trees where he wrote *Our Mutual Friend*. He had five mirrors placed around the walls to reflect every change of light

Charles Dickens in 1865. From a photograph 'taken in England.'
Photo: Dickens House Museum, London.

and a telescope to look out across the countryside.

28

He wrote to an American friend: 'Divers birds sing here all day, and the nightingales all night. The place is lovely and in perfect order . . . My room is up among the branches of the trees; and the birds and butterflies fly in and out and the green branches shoot in at the open windows and the lights and shadows of the clouds come and go with the rest of the company. The scent of the flowers, and indeed of everything that is growing for miles and miles, is most delicious.'

Dickens made many improvements to the house, such as the tiles he had laid in the billiard room to prevent cues from marking the wall. He also lined his study door with a counterfeit library, full of hilariously titled books including:*The Quarrelly Review* in four volumes, *Noah's Arkitecture* in two volumes, *Chickweed, Groundsell* (by the author of *Chickweed), Cockatoo on Perch* and *Hansard's Guide to Refreshing Sleep*.

In 1865, Charles Dickens and Ellen were involved together in a serious train crash in Kent on their return from Boulogne.

Dickens' own deteriorating health was not helped by a marathon reading tour of America in 1867/8. When he returned to England, in April 1868, he went straight to the house he had rented for Ellen Ternan in Peckham, leaving the family remaining at Gad's Hill to guess his whereabouts. When he eventually arrived home, the streets were lined with flags and cheering villagers.

Through all this, Dickens' literary output never faltered. It was a punishing routine of irregular meals, lack of sleep and emotional stress and towards the end of his life his doctor became convinced the demands he had made on himself all his life were now killing him. Dickens knew he had to stop.

This restlessness arose from great inner sadness. Towards the end of his life he wrote of this heartache: 'It is much better to go on and fret, than to stop and fret. As to repose – for some men there's no such thing in this life . . . The old days – the old days! Shall I ever, I wonder, get the frame of mind back as it used to be then? . . . However strange it is to be never at rest, and never satisfied, and ever trying after something that is never reached, and to be always laden with plot and plan and care and worry, how clear it is that it must be, and that one is driven by an irresistible might until the journey is worked out!'

The final reading took place on March 15 1870. It was an emotional occasion. Hundreds of people had gathered to hear for the last time the voices of Scrooge, Cratchit and Bob Weller brought to life by their creator. He had a bad throat and was in pain but the audience cheered themselves hoarse too.

When the applause died down, the tears streaming down his face, Dickens spoke. This time he was not acting: '. . . it would be hypocritical and unfeeling – if I were to disguise that I close this chapter in my life with feelings of very considerable pain . . .. from these garish lights I vanish now for evermore, with a heartfelt, grateful and respectful and affectionate farewell.'

The words of Sidney Carton in *A Tale of Two Cities* could be those of Dickens himself: 'as I draw closer and closer to the end, I travel in the circle, nearer and nearer to the beginning.'

He came home to Gad's Hill, where he worked on *The Mystery of Edwin Drood*. He had just completed a splendid new conservatory and on 8 July 1870, in cheerful mood, he returned to the chalet after lunch and began to write: 'A brilliant morning shines on the old city.'

The words echo the first sentence of his first novel, *The Pickwick Papers:* 'The first ray of light which illumines the gloom . . . '

As Peter Ackroyd says – 'One opening with light and with Rochester, the other closing on the same two notes. Light calling to light, the figure of Dickens bent between them . . . The circle of life.'

At dinner that evening, Georgina asked if he was ill and he replied, 'yes, very ill.' Even so, he proposed to undertake a planned visit to London. He stood up, but became incoherent. She begged him to lie down and he simply said: 'Yes, on the ground.' But as she tried to help he slid from her grasp and became unconscious.

Kate, Charley and Mamie were summoned and Kate recalled the silence of the house in which Dickens had generated so much life and laughter, and so much heartache too. The scent of his favourite geraniums wafted from the conservatory. The next day Georgina sent for Ellen Ternan. In the early evening his breathing faded and tears poured down his cheeks. They were all with him when he died.

When the news that Dickens had died was announced, his death was treated as a national calamity. The *Spectator* eulogised: 'The greatest humorist whom England ever produced – Shakespeare himself certainly not excepted – is gone.' The Italian press lamented in typically theatrical headlines: '*Il nostro Carlo Dickens e morto*' – 'Our Charles Dickens is dead'.

A death mask was made of the man who, in his life, had a horror of masks. Geraniums were placed on his simple oak coffin. A few days after his death the poignant drawing *The Empty Chair* was completed by artist Luke Fildes.

His will was unequivocal and uncharacteristically unflamboyant in its demands: 'I emphatically direct that I be buried in an inexpensive, unostentatious, and strictly private manner; that no public announcement be made of the the time or place of my burial; that at the utmost not more than three plain mourning coaches be employed; and that those who attend my funeral wear no scarf, cloak, black bow, long hat-band or other such revolting absurdity . . . conjure my friends on no account to make me the subject of any monument, memorial, or testimonial whatever . . . ' It was the request of a man who knew exactly how high he stood in the nation's regard.

Dickens was buried in Poets' Corner, Westminster Abbey, and not, as he wished, in the graveyard adjoining Rochester Castle moat. His distraught friend and biographer, John Forster, made extraordinary efforts to protect Dickens' wishes.

In his *Recollections*, Dean Stanley, who was in charge of the funeral arrangements, says: 'Mr Forster was . . . so much overcome by the violence of his grief that he could hardly speak.' He requested that Dickens' wishes about the mourning coaches and ceremonial should be observed. He then asked that no publicity should be given to the time of the funeral.

'Accordingly,' wrote the Dean, 'at six o'clock in the evening I told the Clerk of the Works to prepare the grave. We went into the Abbey and by the dim light chose a spot near Thackeray's bust, and surrounded on various sides by Handel . . . and Sheridan . . . I left him to make the grave and retired to bed. At midnight there came a thundering knock at the door.' It was the *Daily Telegraph*, hot-foot on the trail of a story but the Dean's servant said that he had gone to bed and sent them away.

Next morning at nine, 'a solitary hearse with two mourning coaches drove into Dean's Yard. It attracted no observation whatever . . . The coffin entered with the eight or twelve mourners, and was sunk into the grave . . . It was a beautiful summer morning, and the effect of the almost silent and solitary funeral in the vast space of the Abbey, of this famous writer, whose interment, had it been known, would have drawn thousands to the Abbey, was very striking.'

The grave was left open for three days, during which time the public, including hundreds of children, brought posies, nosegays and hedgerow flowers to place on the coffin. Forster never returned to the Abbey, after what he called 'that fatal day'.

Each year on 9 June, the Dickens Fellowship places a chaplet of geraniums on his tomb in Poets' Corner in Westminster Abbey. A memorial tablet was made for Rochester Cathedral and on the Sunday nearest the date of his death, the Rochester branch also places a chaplet beneath this tablet. For his birthday, in Rochester a cake is cut and 'the Immortal Memory' is toasted at the February meeting.

6

DICKENSIANA

IMMEDIATELY anyone who had known Dickens, heard one of his lectures across a smokey room, or merely shared an affinity for geraniums, jumped on the bandwaggon – and the bandwaggon began to roll.

His novels were dramatised and in 1873 Catherine Dickens, his widow, attended a performance of *Dombey and Son* at the Globe Theatre but had to leave, in tears.

John Forster's definitive and detailed *Life of Dickens* appeared in 1875. It was a gargantuan work, based upon their long-standing personal friendship and his privileged access to letters and family papers.

Dickens' manager, George Dolby, also weighed in with his own reminiscences of life on tour with Dickens. Guides to Dickens country became popular too. *In Kent with Charles Dickens* appeared in 1880, Robert Langton's *Charles Dickens and Rochester* was published in 1880 and in 1888 William R Hughes set off on *A Week's Tramp in Dickens-Land*' for 'health and recreation.' This was published in 1891. According to Hughes, he and his companion 'mixed with . . . domestics, labourers, artizans (*sic*) traders, professional men and scientists.'

There was eventually, of course, a backlash – an outpouring of criticism mainly from fellow writers who disliked Dickens' verbosity, his sentimentality and his unconvincing women. Anthony Trollope had once called him Mr Popular Sentiment. Admonishing critics, in 1906 G.K.Chesterton wrote effusively in the first chapter of his biography: 'If, then you are a pessimist, in reading this story, forego for a little the pleasures of pessimism. Dream for one mad moment that the grass is green. Unlearn that sinister learning that you think so clear; deny that deadly knowledge that you think you know. Surrender the very flower of your culture; give up the very jewel of your pride; abandon hopelessness, all ye who enter here.'

Years later, in 1940, George Orwell, who wrote with witty insight, claimed that Dickens' 'parts are greater than his wholes – rotten architecture but wonderful gargoyles.' He has remained popular with the ordinary reader, because, says Orwell, he is able to express in a comic, simplified and therefore memorable form, the native decency of the common man. Dickens 'voiced the idea of human brotherhood to which nearly everyone responds emotionally.'

Pickwick Clubs proliferated. In the year of his death a Pickwick Cycling Club was born and by 1902 both the Dickens Fellowship and the Boz Club had been founded.

The declared aims of the Fellowship include the wish:

'a) To knit together in a common bond of fellowship lovers of that great master of humour and pathos, Charles Dickens.

'b) To spread the love of humanity, which is the keynote of all his work.

'c) To take such measures as may be expedient to remedy those existing social evils, the amelioration of which would have appealed so strongly to the heart of Charles Dickens.'

Rochester itself also commemorated its association with Dickens. In 1903 a branch of the Dickens Fellowship was inaugurated, with Dean Hole (1819–1904) as President. By 1905 the collected records of the magazine *The Dickensian*, recorded a worldwide readership of 6,500 from Winnipeg to the Gold Coast. Today the Fellowship has about 6,000 members in forty nine branches worldwide and holds an annual international conference.

Members of the Boz Club were eminent men of literature, art and science who met for regular dinners and pilgrimages. On 8 June 1901 the club conducted what was probably the first organised 'perambulation' of Pickwickland. They visited, among other places, The Leather Bottle where they were unable to see Pickwick's bedroom because 'the innkeeper found a couple had turned the key on intruders!'

Edwin Harris (1859–1938), Rochester's own, if sometimes erratic, historian, became the city's self-appointed guide conducting visitors, gratuitously, around the Dickens' sites and writing copiously, pouring out almost as many words in his time as had his idol. He could recite whole

Rochester historian and self appointed tour guide, Edward Harris, with a life-size model. *Photo: Guildhall Museum, Rochester.*

chapters by heart. Mr Harris always claimed that Dickens had rescued him as a boy, when his head became stuck in the railings near Rochester Bridge.

The Rochester Pickwick Club which admits, necessarily, only 'twelve gentlemen' (and no ladies except at Christmas) at any one time, is a comparatively recent formation. It was founded in 1984 by Cyril Baldwin, former auctioneer and genial Pickwick look-alike.

Invitations to the regular dinners are addressed in character – to Mr Samuel Weller or Mr Alfred Jingle. The evenings, unlike those of other Pickwick Clubs, are always in costume and follow a time-honoured snuff-taking formula. Grace precedes a toast to the Immortal Memory and a reading from *Pickwick Papers*.

Throughout the meal, protocol is observed and if any member fails to use the character names of other guests he is fined a bottle of port. Port is always received in the left hand, passed across, anti-clockwise and poured with the right but must not be put down until it has gone full circle. Failure to do so results in another fine – of a bottle of port. The evening concludes with the Loyal Toast.

Mr Dickens himself is the honorary member – watching over proceedings in bust form . These dinners are now held in various venues by invitation – even, on one occasion, in the window of a department store in Tunbridge Wells.

After some years purely as a dining club, the Pickwickians felt the need

The much travelled chalet that was Dickens' hideaway at Gad's Hill is now in the gardens of Eastgate House.
Photo: Rochester Upon Medway City Council.

to fulfil a greater role in the community. They began charity fund raising – appearing at fetes, school sports, cricket matches and, in particular, visiting hospitals.

Every Christmas they are welcomed by the Wisdom Hospice, Rochester, which was opened by the Queen. Mr Pickwick was invited to meet Her Majesty in the High Street and was so unusually overcome that by the time he reached home he had completely forgotten what she said.

Immediately after Dickens' death, Gad's Hill, to the family's concern, was bought by Charley – they felt he could not afford it. The contents were auctioned. Mamie and Georgina stayed on for a time but in 1878 the house was finally sold again and the family moved out.

In 1924 Gad's Hill became a school. Although an extension was added to accommodate pupils, it is surprisingly unchanged from the days when the house echoed to the sounds of 'Venerables' skylarking with his grandchildren. Still there are the upside down horseshoe in the hall, turned to allow luck to escape into the house, and the tiles laid to protect the wall from the over exuberant use of billiard cues.

Dickens' study is now the headmistress's office. The conservatory he finished with such pride just before his death has been carefully restored and is the school dining room. In the garden visitors are shown the graves of Dickens' sherry-drinking canary Dick, 'the best of birds', and Mrs Bouncer, 'the best, the most faithful, the most loving of little dogs.'

In 1992, Miss Posy Barlow, an American admirer of Dickens, funded the restoration of the bell in the cupola on the roof. Today, this is ceremonially rung to announce the arrival of any member of the Dickens family.

The chalet, Dickens' hideaway, was removed to London and was eventually presented to Lord Darnley, who reconstructed it, appropriately, in the flower garden at the back of his mansion, Cobham Hall, Kent.

From Gad's Hill to Cobham had been one of Dickens' favourite walks – described in *Pickwick Papers* 'They emerged upon an open park, with an ancient hall, displaying the quaint and picturesque architecture of Elizabeth's time. Long vistas of stately oaks and elm trees appeared on every side: large herds of deer were cropping the fresh grass; and occasionally a startled hare scoured along the ground with the speed of the shadows thrown by the light clouds, which swept across a sunny landscape like a passing breath of summer.'

Like Gad's Hill, Cobham Hall is an independent school today but is regularly open to the public and is licensed for weddings.

In 1961, the chalet was dismantled and re-erected on its present site at Eastgate House in Rochester High Street, where it forms part of the Dickens Centre. It was in a deplorable condition and was restored by the efforts of the Dickens Fellowship and the then City Council.

The house at 48 Doughty Street, where Dickens lived after his marriage, was converted to a Museum in 1925 and has become the headquarters of the Dickens Fellowship, receiving over 30,000 people yearly. Dickens' birthplace in Portsmouth is also a museum.

In 1991 Charles Dickens' original writing desk became the catalyst for a new charity – aimed at carrying on his crusading work. As she sat at the desk, former Hungarian Countess, Jeanne Marie Wenckheim, wife of Dickens' great great grandson Christopher, who is head of the family today, was inspired to establish the Charles Dickens Heritage Foundation to raise money for the under-privileged. Together with their daughters, Catherine and Lucy, they decided to reproduce and market exact copies of the desk.

The venture foundered at first in Britain. So Jeanne Marie turned to America and the Foundation, run on a voluntary basis by the family, was eventually chartered in North Carolina. Licences were granted both for the reproduction of the desk and the design of other memorabilia – porcelain inns, ornaments and even ceramic Victorian villages, drawn from the novels.

To date, more than $400,000 have been granted to American charities and to organisations serving the young, the elderly, the homeless and the terminally ill. It is Jeanne Marie's dream to establish Hartford, Connecticut, which Dickens had visited twice in his lifetime, as the Dickens Centre in America.

Other descendants of Dickens today find themselves always in demand. 'We have all inherited his love of show business', says great grandson David Dickens who, with his cheery energy and bushy beard, could be Dickens re-incarnated. David Dickens travels the world lecturing, while his son, Gerald, also continues the Dickens tradition with his popular one-man show based on readings from the novels.

7

THE ROCHESTER BOOKS

What a world of gammon and spinnage it is, though, ain't it! Miss Mowcher,
David Copperfield

THERE is hardly a place in and around the City of Rochester upon Medway that does not feature somewhere in Dickens' books. From its earliest appearance as Great Winglebury in *Sketches by Boz*, to its role as the setting for his masterly *The Mystery of Edwin Drood*, Rochester is everywhere. And the counterparts of the characters who move through the pages of his books can be recognised, even today, in the streets and the countryside beyond.

Only three of the major novels were written largely in Rochester: *The Tale of Two Cities* and *Our Mutual Friend*, neither of which feature the city, and *The Mystery of Edwin Drood*, in which it plays such an important role. It lives too in *Pickwick Papers*, briefly in *David Copperfield*, the Christmas Tale of 1854 – *Seven Poor Travellers*, *The Uncommercial Traveller* and in *Great Expectations*.

The ancient magic of Rochester cathedral and its castle, in particular, inspired Dickens and repeatedly cast their spell over his stories. He longed to be buried within their protection in the old cemetery of St Nicholas, once part of the castle moat.

THE CASTLE

'What a study for an antiquarian!' were the very words which fell from Mr Pickwick's mouth, as he applied his telescope to his eye.

'Ah, fine place!' said the stranger, 'glorious pile – frowning walls, tottering arches – dark nooks – crumbling staircases.'

According to William R.Hughes in his 'A Week's Tramp in Dickens-Land', Dickens always took his friends to see the castle and wrote most movingly of it in *Household Words* in 1851.

I climbed the rugged staircase, stopping now and then to peep at great holes where the rafters and floors were once – bare as toothless gums now – or to enjoy glimpses of the Medway through dreary apertures like sockets without eyes: and, looking from the Castle ramparts on the Old Cathedral, and on the crumbling remains of the old Priory, and on the row of staid old red-brick houses where the Cathedral dignitaries live. . . felt quite apologetic to the scene in general for my own juvenility and insignificance.

Rochester Castle. *Photo: Rochester Upon Medway City Council*

Gundulf, a Norman monk, was one of the early building bishops. From 1077, when he became Bishop of Rochester he built its castle, but not the keep, its cathedral and a monastery. He also added the White Tower to the Tower of London.

Photo: Rochester Upon Medway City Council.

THE CATHEDRAL

'Old Cathedral too' said Mr Jingle, in *Pickwick Papers*, 'earthy smell – pilgrims' feet worn away the old steps – little Saxon doors – confessionals like money-takers' boxes at theatres – queer customers those monks . . . '

The formidable strength of the cathedral is also described by the lawyer, Mr Grewgious, in *The Mystery of Edwin Drood*. He peers inside:

'Dear me', said Mr Grewgious, peeping in, 'it's like looking down the throat of Old Time.' Old Time heaved a mouldy sigh from tomb and arch and vault; and gloomy shadows began to deepen in corners; and damps began to rise from green patches of stone; and jewels, cast upon the pavement of the nave from stained glass by the declining sun, began to perish.

SKETCHES BY BOZ
FROM 1836

THE *Sketches* were a series of journalistic essays looking at the world around Dickens. They were sometimes reflective, sometimes humorous, usually perceptive, although Dickens himself wrote critically of these first attempts at authorship: 'I am conscious of their being often extremely crude and ill-considered and bearing obvious marks of haste and inexperience.'

In *The Great Winglebury Duel*, Alexander Trott is trying to avoid a duel with his rival-in-love, Horace Hunter. Rochester High Street, the proposed site of the duel, is described much as it is today as a 'long straggling, quiet High Street, with a great black and white clock and a small red town hall half way up – a market place – a cage – an assembly room – a church – a bridge – a chapel – a theatre – a library – an inn – a pump and a post office.'

THE POSTHUMOUS PAPERS OF THE PICKWICK CLUB
PART PUBLISHED FROM MARCH 1836

THE *Posthumous Papers of the Pickwick Club* was written as a serial in the *Monthly Magazine* and the first episode was published on 31 March – two days before Dickens' wedding. By the time the last chapter had appeared the magazine sales had rocketed to 40,000 copies monthly.

Match box cover of 1867. *Photo: Dickens House Musuem, London.*

Mr Pickwick was a phenomenon, in a benign imaginary world full of people with whom men and women of all classes could identify.

Immediately there was a commercial bonanza. The *Pickwick Comic Almanack*, *Pickwick Abroad* and the *Pickwick Treasury of Wit* were among books that appeared. Retailers sold Pickwick hats, Pickwick coats, Pickwick cigars and teapots and Sam Weller corduroys. By 1840 fans in Christchurch, New Zealand, had formed what they claim was the world's first Pickwick Club.

THE STORY as it affects Rochester

Samuel Pickwick, middle-aged, retired and naively jovial President of the Pickwick Club, confounds its members with a learned paper entitled *Speculations on the Source of the Hampstead Ponds with some Observations on the Theory of Tittlebats.*

As a result he forms the Corresponding Branch of the Club and sets out from London with three other members on a journey of scientific and cultural investigation. His companions are the would-be, but unsuccessful, sportsman Nathaniel Winkle, the poetic Augustus Snodgrass and the elderly roué, Tracy Tupman.

First stop is the Medway towns and their adventures begin at the Bull Inn in Rochester. Here a mysterious actor, Alfred Jingle, persuades Tracy Tupman to borrow the sleeping Nathaniel Winkle's evening dress and to accompany him to the Assembly Ball.

It is a decision that results in an alleged insult to the balding Dr Slammer, surgeon to the 97th (based on Dickens' uncle James Lamert, an army staff doctor.) There follows a case of mistaken identity leading to the notorious duel at Fort Pitt, in which the bemused Mr Winkle finds himself wrongly facing the armed wrath of the outraged Dr Slammer.

The staircase of the Bull Inn, Rochester, where Dr Slammer defied Mr Jingle.
Photo: R L Ratcliffe

So, from Fort Pitt the friends proceed to a military review on The Lines at Chatham, where they meet a country squire, Mr Wardle, his spinster sister Rachel, his daughters and their greedy fat servant Joe.

The friends are invited to their manor eight miles away at Dingley Dell, Mr Pickwick undertaking the journey in a chaise, inexperienced Mr Winkle on horseback.

The horse no sooner beheld Mr Pickwick advancing towards him with the chaise whip in his hand, than he exchanged the rotary motion in which he had previously indulged, for a retrograde movement of so very determined a character, that it at once drew Mr Winkle, who was still at the end of the bridle at a rather quicker rate than fast walking, in the direction from which they had just come. Mr Pickwick ran to his assistance, but the faster Mr Pickwick ran forward, the faster the horse ran backward there was a great scraping of feet, and kicking up of dust; and at last Mr Winkle, his arms being nearly pulled out of their sockets, fairly let go his hold. The horse paused, stared, shook his head, turned round and quietly trotted home to Rochester leaving Mr Winkle and Mr Pickwick gazing on each other with countenances of blank dismay.

Once arrived at Dingley Dell, the unfortunate Mr Winkle goes shooting, misses his bird and shoots Tracy Tupman in the arm. Miss Rachel Wardle, anxious for marriage and not one to miss an opportunity, embarks on a romance between the victim and herself. But he is outmanoeuvred by the actor, Alfred Jingle, who elopes with her to London, hotly pursued by the Pickwickians.

THE PLACES

THE MEDWAY TOWNS

The principal productions of these towns . . . appear to be soldiers, sailors, Jews, chalk, shrimps, officers and dockyard men. The commodities chiefly exposed for sale in the public streets are marine stores, hard-bake, apples, flat fish, and oysters. The streets present a lively and animated appearance occasioned chiefly by the conviviality of the military . . . The consumption of tobacco in these towns . . . must be very great, and the smell which pervades the streets must be exceedingly delicious to those who are extremely fond of smoking.

A superficial traveller might object to the dirt, which is their leading characteristic; but to those who view it as an indication of traffic and commercial prosperity, it is truly gratifying.

THE BULL, High Street, Rochester.

'Good house – nice beds'. Originally this eighteenth century coaching inn was called the Bull on the Hoope but was renamed the Royal Victoria and Bull after the future Queen Victoria stayed there before her Coronation.

It was a long room with crimson-covered benches, and wax candles in glass chandeliers. The musicians were confined in an elevated den . . . Two card tables were made up in the adjoining card-room, and two pairs of old ladies, and a corresponding number of old gentlemen, were executing whist therein.

The ballroom, with its chandelier, remains and the Rochester Pickwick Club still meets for dinner upstairs.

ROCHESTER BRIDGE

The medieval stone bridge of Mr Pickwick's day was far removed from the road/rail constructions in existence today. This was then still the only

In the foreground is Rochester's medieval stone bridge and behind it Cubitt's cast iron bridge opened in 1856. *Photo: Fine Art Studios, Strood.*

45

way over the Medway into Rochester and the views it offered were spectacular. So many of Dickens' characters paused upon the bridge.

Mr Pickwick: 'On either side, the banks of the Medway, covered with cornfields and pastures, with here and there a windmill, or a distant church, stretched away as far as the eye could see, presenting a rich and varied landscape . . . The river, reflecting the clear blue of the sky, glistened and sparkled as it flowed noiselessly on; and the oars of the fishermen dipped into the water with a clear and liquid sound. . . '

FORT PITT

The fields of Fort Pitt run above the New Road in Rochester and have a superb view of the Medway and the City. They contain the remains of Napoleonic fortifications and it is here that Dr Slammer and Mr Winkle met for their duel.

If the principal tower of Rochester Castle had suddenly walked from its foundation, and stationed itself opposite the coffee-room window, Mr Winkle's surprise would have been as nothing.. 'All right' said Mr Snodgrass. 'Be steady and wing him'. It occurred to Mr Winkle that this advice was very like that which by-standers invariably give to the smallest boy in a street fight, namely: 'Go in and win'– an admirable thing to recommend, if you only know how to do it . . . Mr Winkle was always remarkable for extreme humanity. It is conjectured that his unwillingness to hurt a fellow creature intentionally was the cause of his shutting his eyes when he arrived at the fatal spot; and that the circumstance of his eyes being closed, prevented his observing the very extraordinary and unaccountable demeanour of Doctor Slammer. That gentleman started, stared, retreated, rubbed his eyes, stared again, and finally, shouted 'Stop, stop! . . . that's not the man.

THE LINES, Chatham

This is a massive fortified network of tunnels, walls, batteries, forts and ditches, started in 1756 to protect Britain from the French. Today the weekend manoeuvres and gun battles that take place in full eighteenth century military dress are educational and not real.

'It is indeed a noble and a brilliant sight,' said Mr Snodgrass, in whose bosom a blaze of poetry was rapidly bursting forth, 'to see the gallant defenders of their country drawn up in brilliant array before its peaceful citizens; their faces beaming – not with warlike ferocity, but with civilised gentleness; their eyes

46

flashing – not with the rude fire of rapine or revenge, but with the soft light of humanity and intelligence . . . '

The military bands struck up altogether; the horses stood upon two legs each, cantered backwards, and whisked their tails about in all directions; the dogs barked, the mob screamed, the troops recovered . . . Mr Pickwick had been so fully occupied in falling about and disentangling himself, miraculously, from between the legs of horses, that he had not enjoyed sufficient leisure to observe the scene before him.

THE LEATHER BOTTLE, Cobham

The Leather Bottle 'a clean commodious village ale house' was the timber framed inn where Dickens stayed on several occasions and to which he brought Mr Pickwick. Today it has changed very little and is rich in Dickensiana.

DAVID COPPERFIELD
PUBLISHED MAY 1849

THIS is Dickens' self-acknowledged autobiography in which David visits the city of Rochester, briefly, on his journey to Aunt Betsy Trotwood.

Dickens' own personality is reflected throughout the book – his loneliness, his exaggerated, child's memory of adult betrayal, his failure with women and the unbearable pain of losing loved ones.

Dickens wrote to John Forster: 'Oh my dear Forster, if I were to say half of what Copperfield makes me feel tonight, how strangely, even to you I should be turned inside out! I seem to be sending part of myself into the shadowy world.'

He remembers the inner despair of that day when he left behind his childhood – and Rochester – as David too looks back:

Long miles of road then opened out before my mind: and, toiling on, I saw a ragged wayworn boy, forsaken and neglected, who should come to call even the heart now beating against mine, his own.

It is a story of star-crossed love, which was begun shortly after the death of Dickens' sister Fanny, in 1848. Her crippled son too, died from a broken heart, a few months later. Fact and fiction merge throughout David Copperfield. Dickens named his newest baby daughter, born in

1850, Dora, after the ill-starred heroine of the book. And then poignantly, like Dora, the baby died. The character of Dora revived in Dickens the passion he felt for Maria Beadnell when his hopes were still so high.

The young Charles Dickens from a miniature by Rosa Emma Drummond.
Photo: Dickens House Museum, London.

She was more than human to me. She was a Fairy, a Sylph. I don't know what she was – anything that no-one ever saw, and everything that everybody ever wanted.

At the time of writing, Dickens eldest son, Charley, was exactly the same age as was Dickens when his mother sent him to work in the blacking factory and his own unhappy memories of that time came flooding back. For the first time he allowed his feelings to flow, writing honestly of the degradation he had felt.

D C IS C D – he said. 'I never can approach the book with perfect composure (it had such perfect possession of me when I wrote it.)' The story was not an immediate success and was only later hailed as his greatest work.

THE STORY

David's father dies before he is born. When his mother remarries he goes with Peggotty his nurse to stay with her brother Daniel, who lives in an upturned boat in Yarmouth, with two adopted orphans, Ham and Little Em'ly.

On his return David is bullied by his step father, bites him in self defence and is sent away to school in Blackheath, where he makes friends with James Steerforth. While he is there his mother dies and he is sent to work, lodging with Mr and Mrs Micawber. Mr Micawber is always waiting for 'something to turn up'.

But when Mr Micawber finds himself in the debtors' prison and David decides to run away to Dover to find his Aunt, Betsy Trotwood. He is robbed of his luggage and forced to walk, passing through Rochester on the way. Betsy Trotwood adopts David and sends him to school.

After leaving school, David meets Steerforth again and they visit

TRAMPS

The essay on tramps describes the countryside around Gad's Hill –
now largely vanished beneath industrial development and urbanisation.

I have my eye on a piece of Kentish road, bordered on either side by a wood, and
having on one hand, between the road dust and the trees, a skirting patch of
grass. Wild flowers grow in abundance on this spot, and it lies high and airy,
with a distant river stealing steadily away to the ocean, like a man's life . . . Bless
the place, I love the ashes of the vagabond fires that have scorched its grass!
What tramp children do I see here, attired in a handful of rags, making a gym-
nasium of the shafts of the cart, making a feather-bed of the flints and brambles,
making a toy of the hobbled old horse who is not much more like a horse than
any cheap toy would be!

DULLBOROUGH TOWN

In Dullborough Town the *Traveller* makes the painful discovery that
nothing matches the memory of the child. He meets the old greengrocer
who had figured so largely in his young life – to find that his hero has
long forgotten him.

I had no right, I reflected, to be angry with the greengrocer for his want of
interest; I was nothing to him: whereas he was the town, the cathedral, the
bridge, the river, my childhood, and a large slice of my life, to me.

He also returns to the cornfields where he had played, only to find:

. . . the station had swallowed up the playing field. I looked in again over the
low wall at the scene of departed glories. Here, in the haymaking time, had I
been delivered from the dungeons of Seringapatam, an immense pile (of hay-
cock) by my countrymen, the victorious British (boy next door and his two
cousins) and had been recognised with ecstacy by my affianced one (Miss
Green) who had come all the way from England (second house in the terrace)
to ransom me and marry me. . . there was no comfort in the theatre. It was mys-
teriously gone, like my own youth . . . the town had shrunk fearfully since I was
a child there. I found the High Street little better than a lane . . . Ah, who was I
that I should quarrel with the town for being changed to me, when I, myself,
had come back so changed to it! All my early readings and early imaginations
dated from this place and I took them away, so full of innocent construction
and guileless belief, and I brought them back so worn and torn, so much the
wiser and so much the worse

THE ROYAL NAVAL DOCKYARD, CHATHAM

When Dickens was a boy Chatham Dockyard was brimming over with energy and action, for the Royal Navy was being overhauled and refitted for the great and glorious days of Victorian expansion. *The Uncommercial Traveller* remembers those glorious days:

Ding, clash, dong, Bang, boom, rattle, clash, boom, rattle, clash, Bang, clink, bang, dong, bang, clatter, Bang, Bang, BANG. What on earth is this?

This is or soon will be the *Achilles* iron armour-plated ship. Twelve hundred men are working at her now, twelve hundred men working on stages over her sides, over her bows, over her stern, under her keel, between her decks, down in her hold, within her and without, crawling and creeping into the finest curves of her lines, wherever it is possible for men to twist. Twelve hundred hammerers, measurers, caulkers, armourers, forgers, smiths, shipwrights, twelve hundred dingers, clashers, dongers, rattlers, clinkers, bangers, bangers, bangers.

GREAT EXPECTATIONS
PART PUBLISHED FROM 1860

THIS book belongs almost entirely to Rochester. It is, on the surface, a story of the love of a man for a woman who has no heart; two people whose lives have been blighted by their youth. But beneath its windswept greyness is once again a complex and sensitive portrayal of the fears of childhood and a harsh and extraordinarily honest self-exploration by Dickens of his own disappointments with himself. It was a story, he said, 'so cold, so lonely.'

THE STORY

The fearsome convict, Magwitch, looms out of the mist in the church-yard at Cooling and frightens the boy Philip Pirrip. 'Pip' as he is known, lives with his sister and blacksmith brother-in-law, Joe Gargery.

Magwitch has escaped from the hulks and Pip feeds him secretly. Magwitch never forgets. Years later when he becomes a wealthy man in Australia, Magwitch decides to share his fortune anonymously with the grown-up Pip.

Meanwhile, Pip has been introduced to the elderly Miss Havisham, living in a house which has remained exactly as it was on the day she was jilted. She is dressed, still, in her bridal gown and never leaves the darkened room which has been her home for years.

Pip falls hopelessly in love with Estella, who was adopted by Miss Havisham. But Estella has been trained to 'wreak revenge on all the male sex' – Pip included. Pip learns from Miss Havisham's lawyer, Mr Jaggers, (who also, unbeknown, acts for Magwitch), that he, Pip, has 'great expectations'. Out of the blue Magwitch returns from Australia, risking death, and Pip learns that his unknown benefactor is not, as he suspected, Miss Havisham but Magwitch himself. After an initially hostile reaction, Pip becomes very fond of Magwitch.

He learns that Jaggers' housekeeper is in fact, Estella's mother and then, dramatically, that Magwitch is her father. Pip goes to see Miss Havisham and as he is leaving sees her wedding dress catch fire and rushes back to rescue the old lady. But he is too late and she dies. Magwitch is injured and dies in prison having been condemned to death.

The ragstone tombstones in Cooling churchyard where 'Pip's parents and all his brothers were buried.' *Photo: Rochester Upon Medway City Council.*

In despair, Pip goes abroad for ten years and returns to find Estella an unhappy widow, still living at Satis House. Their future is never revealed.

I took her hand in mine, and we went out of the ruined place; and, as the morning mists had risen long ago when I first left the forge, so, the evening mists were rising now, and . . . I saw no shadow of another parting from her.

PIP'S ROCHESTER

THE CHURCHYARD, Cooling.

There are, in all, thirteen small ragstone tombstones, shaped like coffins, in Cooling churchyard and not, as Dickens mentions, just five. Pip describes his earliest memories of that ghostly place, where his parents and all his brothers lie buried:

At such a time I found out, for certain, that this bleak place overgrown with nettles was the churchyard; . . . and that . . . beyond the churchyard, intersected with dykes, and mounds, and gates with scattered cattle feeding on it, was the marshes; and that the low leaden line beyond was the river; and that the distant savage lair, from which the wind was rushing, was the sea; and that the small bundle of shivers growing afraid of it all, and beginning to cry, was Pip.

THE MARSH

From that 'savage lair' where little Pip shrank amongst the gravestones, emerged the terrible figure of Magwitch.

A fearful man all in coarse grey, with a great iron on his leg. A man with no hat, and with broken shoes, and with an old rag tied round his head. A man who had been soaked in water, and smothered in mud, and lamed by stones, and cut by flints, and stung by nettles, and torn by briers; who limped and shivered, and glared and growled and whose teeth chattered in his head as he seized me by the chin.

THE GUILDHALL, High Street, Rochester.

It was to the Guildhall that Pip came with Joe Gargery, to be articled as an apprentice.

The hall was a queer place I thought, with higher pews in it than a church – and mighty Justices leaning back in chairs, with folded arms, or taking snuff, or going to sleep, or writing, or reading the newspapers . . . and with some shining black portraits on the walls, which my unartistic eye regarded as a composition of hardbake and sticking plaster. There, in a corner my indentures were duly signed and attested, and I was 'bound'.

UNCLE PUMBLECHOOK'S HOUSE, 154 High Street

Photo: Rochester Upon Medway City Council.

The timber framed building directly across the High Street from Eastgate House was the home of Pip's Uncle Pumblechook.

The premises were, said Pip: 'of a peppercorny and farinaceous character, as the premises of a corn chandler and seedsman should be.'

High up, between the gables is the window of Pip's attic where he complains of its 'sloping roof which was so low in the corner where the bedstead was, that I calculated the tiles as being within a foot of my eyelashes.'

SATIS HOUSE

The Satis House in *Great Expectations* is, confusingly, not the actual Satis House in Bakers Walk now used by the King's School, but the impressive red brick Restoration House in Crow Lane. Dickens, as he so often did, simply transposed the names.

This is Restoration House in Crow Lane, which Dickens made the Satis House in Great Expectations.
Photo:Rochester Upon Medway City Council.

I crossed the staircase landing, and entered the room she indicated. From that room, too, the daylight was completely excluded . . . A fire had been lately kindled in the damp old fashioned grate, and it was more disposed to go out than to burn up, and the reluctant smoke which hung in the room seemed colder than the clearer air – like our own marsh mist. Certain wintry branches of candles on the high chimney piece faintly lighted the chamber; or, it would be more expressive to say, faintly troubled its darkness . . .

The most prominent object was a long table with a tablecloth spread on it, as if a feast had been in preparation when the house and the clocks all stopped together. An epergne or centre-piece of some kind was in the middle of this cloth; it was so heavily overhung with cobwebs that its form was quite indistinguishable; and, as

I looked along the yellow expanse out of which I remember its seeming to grow, like a black fungus, I saw speckled-legged spiders with blotchy bodies running home to it . . . as if some circumstance of the greatest public importance had just transpired in the spider community. I heard the mice too, rattling behind the panels . . . But, the blackbeetles took no notice of the agitation, and groped about the hearth in a ponderous elderly way, as if they were short-sighted and hard of hearing and not on terms with one another.

THE BLUE BOAR

There is, confusingly, a small guest house recently re-named the Blue Boar in Rochester High Street. But when young Pip was treated to a slap-up meal after being bound as an apprentice, it was the Bull Inn, now the Royal Victoria and Bull, not the Blue Boar which Dickens described as the scene of their celebration. After the meal there was entertainment:

Mr Wopsle gave us Collins's Ode, and threw his blood-stained sword in thunder down, with such effect, that a waiter came in and said 'The commercials underneath sent up their compliments, and it wasn't the Tumblers' Arms.'

OUR MUTUAL FRIEND
PART PUBLISHED FROM 1864

THIS was one of the Rochester-written novels – a moody, misty, but often very funny, novel set around the river (Thames) and its people. Its underlying message is to highlight the iniquities of the Poor Law and the Ragged Schools and especially Dickens' real concern about the exploitation of children.

THE MYSTERY OF EDWIN DROOD
1870 BUT UNFINISHED

EDWIN DROOD was conceived as a short novel to be published in twelve parts. The poet Longfellow claimed when he read it that 'it is certainly one of his most beautiful works, if not the most beautiful of all.'

Dickens had just written the last part of the sixth instalment when he died in June 1870. He left no notes and no indication about the outcome of the story – although it is said that he offered to reveal all to Queen Victoria during an audience in March 1870. She was not interested.

John Forster claimed that Dickens intended the story to be that of a nephew murdered by his uncle, with the last chapter set in the condemned cell. But since Dickens' death many authors have added their own suggested endings.

The book is set London and in Cloisterham – Rochester, where, at the time, one Edwin Trood was landlord of Dickens' local public house, the Falstaff Inn at Gad's Hill.

THE STORY

Edwin Drood is a young man, whose father's dying wish was for him to marry the schoolgirl Rosa Bud, now a pupil of Miss Twinkleton's Academy for young ladies. Neither Rosa nor Edwin, good friends as they are, want to develop their friendship in this way, but they agree to say nothing in public. Edwin's guardian and uncle John Jasper, who is the opium-eating master of the cathedral choir, is is love with her. So is the mysterious Neville Landless, newly arrived from Ceylon with his equally mysterious twin sister, who has been known to dress as a man.

Not surprisingly, they are all very troubled by Edwin's apparently cavalier attitude to Rosa. The lawyer, and Rosa's guardian, Mr Grewgious, is also worried about Edwin and gives him a ring which, he says, should be presented to Rosa when they do become engaged, or returned to him.

On Christmas Eve, Neville Landless and Edwin meet with Jasper to try and sort out their differences. But on his way home Edwin disappears. Landless is questioned but released and then Edwin's watch and shirt pin are found caught in the timbers of Cloisterham Weir. A stranger, calling himself 'Datchery', arrives apparently to keep an eye on Mr Jasper.

But Dickens died, tantalisingly before the reader is told who Datchery really is – or what happened to Edwin Drood.

EDWIN DROOD'S ROCHESTER

An ancient city Cloisterham, and no meet dwelling place for any one with hankerings after the noisy world. A monotonous, silent city, deriving an earthy flavour throughout from its Cathedral crypt, and so abounding in vestiges of monastic graves that the Cloisterham children grow small salad in the dust of abbots and abbesses. . .

A brilliant morning shines on the old city. Its antiquities and ruins are surpassingly beautiful, with the lusty ivy gleaming in the sun, and the rich trees waving in the balmy air. Changes of glorious light from moving boughs, songs of birds, scents from gardens, woods . . . penetrate into the cathedral, subdue its earthly odour, and preach the Resurrection and the Life.

THE NUNS' HOUSE, High Street.

Eastgate House, 'a venerable brick edifice', is now the Dickens Centre. Dickens knew Eastgate House as a girls' school and in *Edwin Drood* it became the Nuns' House, Miss Twinkleton's Seminary for Young Ladies.

The house front is so old and worn, and the brass plate is so shining and staring that the general result has reminded imaginative strangers of a battered old beau with a large modern eye-glass stuck in his blind eye.

MINOR CANON CORNER

Dickens renamed Minor Canon Row Minor Canon Corner. It remains a backwater of nineteenth century terraced homes for church officials, sheltered behind the cathedral.

Minor Canon Row. *Photo: Rochester Upon Medway City Council.*

It was here that the Reverend Septimus Crisparkle lived with his mother, celebrated for her wonderful home-made pickles, jams, biscuits and cordials.

Minor Canon Corner was a quiet place in the shadow of the cathedral, which the cawing of the rooks, the echoing footsteps of rare passers, the sound of the cathedral bell, or the roll of the cathedral organ, seemed to render more quiet than absolute silence.

It was here also that the portentous Luke Honeythunder caused 'a most doleful breakdown' at a party attended by Miss Twinkleton and Rosa Bud with Edwin Drood at the piano.

MR JASPER'S GATEHOUSE

The lopsided gatehouse, home to Mr John Jasper, was one of the old monastery precinct gates. It is now known as Chertsey's Gate and is a private house. At other times it has been known as Cemetery Gate and College Gate.

A certain awful hush pervades the ancient pile, the cloisters and the churchyard after dark. . . One might fancy that the tide of life was stemmed by Mr Jasper's own Gatehouse. The murmur of the tide is heard beyond; but no wave passes the archway, over which his lamp burns red behind the curtain, as if the building were a Lighthouse.

Straight ahead is Chertsey's Gate. The building on the left was demolished in 1891 for road widening.
Photo: Guildhall Museum, Rochester.

TOPE'S HOUSE, High Street.

Neighbour to Mr Jasper was Mr Tope, chief verger and showman, 'accustomed to be very high with excursion parties'. His wife waited on Mr Jasper and let out rooms in his house when they were needed. She arranged the visit of Mr Datchery. Tope's House is now a restaurant.

MR SAPSEA'S HOUSE, High Street.

Dickens places the home of Auctioneer, Mr Thomas Sapsea, 'the purest jackass in Cloisterham' in the same premises as Uncle Pumblechook in 'Great Expectations'. Today it is an estate agents.

Dickens commented that the building had been modernised over the years as people found that they 'preferred air and light to fever and plague.'

THE MONKS' VINEYARD

Behind the Cathedral is The Vines. It was formerly a vineyard and is today a pleasant open space in the heart of the city. The path which intersects it with gates at either end is where Edwin sauntered with Rosa Bud as they discussed their future (or not) together.

'Can't you see a happy future?' For certain neither of them could see a happy present, as the gate opens and closes, and one goes in and the other goes away.

Costumed characters are everywhere at festival time – with impromptu happenings like this to entertain the crowds. *Photo: Medway News.*

The paddle steamer *Kingswear Castle* bound for Rochester with a full complement of passengers to view the festival finale. *Photo: Rochester Upon Medway City Council.*

9

THE DICKENS
FESTIVAL

Wonderful games, wonderful unanimity, wonderful happiness.
A Christmas Carol

THE first Dickens Festival, in February 1912, was organised by the Dickens Fellowship as a Centenary Week to celebrate the author's birth. The official programme, price one penny, included a costume ball and a costume carnival at the County Ice Rink, with 'twenty handsome prizes'. Schools were given a half day holiday and 500 poor children were offered tea by Messrs Hoppers the 'well known bakers.'

Not till 1931 did the City put on its party clothes again for a Civic Week at the end of June. The Rochester Historical Pageant and Industrial Exhibition was a spectacular affair organised by a total of twenty eight committees. Its aim was to harness history to the commercial and industrial development of Rochester. Prince George, who became King George VI, consented to open celebrations on Royal Day.

The pageant covered the story of the city from Roman times in eight episodes. A cast of hundreds was selected from local groups and organisations such as the Boy Scouts, the School of Military Engineering and pensioners. Dame Sybil Thorndike, the celebrated actress, was invited to play the Spirit of Rochester. She had lived in Minor Canon Row as a girl, between 1884 to 1892 and had been a pupil at the Grammar School.

The final episode – Dickens Day – focused on Dickens' last view of Rochester and this last event of the Festival was attended by Dickens' son, Sir Henry Fielding Dickens.

In 1950 the local press revealed Rochester City Council's plan to stage an even bigger and better Dickens Festival Pageant in June 1951. The intention was 'to put forward the City's claims to Dickens in front of the world.' Plans were made for a worldwide scriptwriters' competition with a large cash prize. Two thousand actors were to be given parts. Twenty men took two months and forty miles of tubing, erecting seating for the arena in the castle grounds. Celebrities, including Dame Sybil again, were invited – and came.

But it rained. Of the expected 85,000 revellers, fewer than 19,000 turned out. Most people listened to the opening on the BBC radio's Light Programme, having assumed they would not get tickets, which were also rather expensive. The pageant made a loss of nearly £6,000 – a crippling amount in those days and a hard lesson learned.

Between 31 May and 2 June 1979 the City Council tried again, this time with such spectacular results that the Festival has been repeated annually, by popular demand, ever since. Perhaps the public taste for Dickens had been given a boost by film and television adaptations of his works. Lionel Bart's musical *Oliver* made such songs as *Food, Glorious Food* hit tunes of the time and the demand for Dickens' books was greater than ever.

Plans for the first three day Festival were low key and included a grand parade, a Victorian cricket match, walking tours in the countryside and a street market. Everyone had a great time and although only a few dozen local people wore costume, the idea of dressing up caught on with Dickensian enthusiasm and energy.

Actor and London tour guide, Alec Gifford, remembers that first event. He was a student, fresh from drama school. 'I offered to do some dramatised readings from Dickens and they liked the idea. I have been back every year. There is a great sense of community spirit and fun.'

Dennis Hammond was also part of that original planning team. 'From the beginning we wanted to make this an event for local people,' he said.

Today the greatly increased pre-publicity and television coverage – four crews attend – means that some 200,000 people now come from all over the country and from abroad for the four day festival.

A team of only four, in the Civic Centre office overlooking the Medway, co-ordinates and perfects the practical arrangements. This team enables the tiny city to absorb painlessly all these extra visitors and helps them to explore the surrounding sights and countryside.

The Rochester Pickwick Club, founded in 1984 by former auctioner and Pickwick look-alike Cyril Baldwin. *Photo: Rochester Upon Medway City Council.*

It is a mammoth task which begins the day after each Festival ends and continues until the next. The core events remain much the same from year to year – the Mistletoe Ball, the Pickwick Express, which ferries visitors from London, and the spectacular finale. But new ideas are always welcome. Feeding the ravenous hordes is a major udertaking and the team must work with the Environmental Health authorities. Additional outside contractors are needed to fill the seemingly bottomless pit. Food nearly always runs out.

Everyone must be on site on the Monday prior to the Thursday opening, and there is not a bed free in the city. Extra electricity must be laid on, toilets arranged and the forty five fully trained stewards at work each day must be briefed on their responsibilities. They help to create a safe and healthy environment, caring for the welfare of the public. They monitor crowd behaviour, act as hosts and guides and liaise with the police to ensure the highest possible standards of safety. A park and ride scheme has been introduced to ease the notorious bottlenecks into the City.

At 8.50.a.m. on the Saturday, the Pickwick Special leaves Rochester with Mr Pickwick and the Mayor on board, to meet up with some 400 passengers in Victorian dress, assembled at Victoria Station, where they are entertained by the *Kent Messenger* Pipe Band.

Of course there are hiccups. Everyone remembers the year that the train pulled in to platform one – instead of platform seven. Waiting passengers in their Dickensian finery were shepherded through the surprised week-ending crowds to take their seats for a jolly singsong ride to Rochester in time for the Grand Parade.

On arrival, visitors walk into a city centre which has stepped back into the nineteenth century. The Town Crier welcomes them to streets and shops thronged with men, women and wide-eyed children in Victorian mood. Flower sellers, entertainers, urchins. Many tourists too fall in with the spirit of the event and arrive in costume.

Mr Pickwick strides the streets with Her Majesty, Queen Victoria. There is croquet on the lawn, a duel at The Vines and firemen with hand-cart, hose and shiny brass trimmings, in their turn of century costumes and magnificent helmets. The hurdy-gurdy plays, handbells can be heard and the pipe band frog marches Magwitch to the hulks, whilst the children are entertained to a workhouse tea party – with gruel.

For four days there is a touch of *Rhia Rhama Rhoos* magic in the air. The increasingly elaborate costumes are ready – often after weeks of painstaking work and eye for detail – as revellers take on their roles. Some are so enthusiastic that they even change costumes during the day. Making-up can take an hour or more.

A few key characters are 'booked' by the organisers from year to year. Fagin, Mr Pickwick, Bill Sikes, Miss Havisham are all well-known local 'celebrities' but most people – visitors included – dress as they please, in Victorian style.

Dickens' own stories are dramatised throughout the festival but in addition there are usually performances of all the entertainments he loved – Harlequinade, the circus, the music hall, Punch and Judy, illusion and escapology.

On the Sunday, Rochester Cathedral is the setting for a Memorial Service and the congregation, many still in costume, watches the wreath-laying ceremony performed by the Dickens Fellowship. Even this more solemn occasion would give Dickens cause to chuckle. The memorial to his friend Dean Hole, who died in 1904, was inconveniently sited in front of the Dickens' memorial plaque until this was moved in 1993. So, for all those years, the Fellowship performed a somewhat undignified manoeuvre to lay the chaplet on his memorial and the congregation could not see. . .

On the Saturday and Sunday evenings there is an explosive extravaganza. This combines all the technical wizardry of a modern *son et lumiere* spectacular, with a traditional firework finale, which can be seen from the Esplanade, the Civic Centre or by passengers aboard the specially commissioned *Kingswear Castle* paddle steamer.

Each year there is a different Dickensian theme. Imagine the sinister sound of the tumbrils approaching, the shadowy infamous figure of Madame Defarge, knitting as the condemned men and women approach the guillotine. This is *The Tale of Two Cities* as seen from the banks of the Medway and around the castle keep. The lonely, spotlit figure of Sidney Carton climbs the steps towards the executioner and then, with chilling theatrical effect in full view of the disbelieving audience, his head is severed.

Another year large puppets were silhouetted on the castle walls, followed by a re-enactment of *Dickens' Dream*, bringing together many of the characters from his books, against a full orchestral background.

An engraving by Alfred Bryan after a photograph by Gurney, published in
Moonshine **in December 1888.**
Photo: Dickens House Museum, London.

10

A DICKENSIAN CHRISTMAS

'God bless us everyone!' said Tiny Tim, the last of all. *A Christmas Carol.*

When Queen Victoria came to the throne in 1837, Christmas as we know it hardly existed. Father Christmas was little more than a pagan relic, portrayed in the magazine Punch as a Bacchanalian reveller, glass in hand. The birth of Christ was a not very widely observed, one day, religious festival – no more.

However, the first known description of the genial Father Christmas figure had appeared in Washington Irving's *History of New York* in 1809. But not till 1822 was St Nicholas (Santa Claus) bringer of toys, in a sleigh pulled by reindeer, launched on the American public in Clement C. Moore's poem *The Night Before Christmas*.

In Britain a collision of social changes in the early nineteenth century meant that December 25 was about to be relaunched – not only as a religious celebration but also as the springboard for a season of parties, presents for the children and plum pudding. Christmas cards appeared in 1846, crackers ten years later.

Queen Victoria, Prince Albert and Charles Dickens were probably independently but jointly responsible for setting the snowball rolling through the nineteenth century in Britain. The Royal couple, with their nine children, promoted the concept of family togetherness.

Dickens loved children. He wanted them to be happy. Dickens, the magician and the entertainer, dreaming of his snow-spangled country Christmases in Chatham, sprinkled the season with a magic it did not previously have – and he gave it to children.

The Dickens Christmas is Rochester's way of honouring that gift.

Dickens first wrote of Christmas when he described the hilarious goings-on at Manor Farm, Dingley Dell where members of the Pickwick Club were enjoying the festivities.

In all sorts of recesses, and on all kinds of brackets, stood massive old silver candlesticks with four branches each. The carpet was up, the candles burned bright, the fire blazed and crackled on the hearth, and merry voices and light-hearted laughter rang through the room. If any of the old English yeoman had turned into fairies when they died, it was just the place in which they would have held their revels.

There were fiddlers, a harp and dancing too but most of all there was mistletoe at Dingley Dell.

Mr Winkle kissed the young lady with the black eyes, and Mr Snodgrass kissed Emily, and Mr Weller, not being particular about the form of being under the mistletoe kissed Emma and the other female servants, just as he caught them. As to the poor relations, they kissed everybody, not even excepting the plainer portions of the young lady visitors, who, in their excessive confusion, ran right under the mistletoe, as soon as it was hung up, without knowing it! .....before Mr Pickwick distinctly knew what was the matter, he was surrounded by the whole body, and kissed by every one of them.

In 1840 Queen Victoria married Prince Albert and Dickens wrote his first Christmas story, *A Christmas Carol*. This stressed the obligation of grown-ups to ensure that children had a good and happy time. Dickens said that he 'wept and laughed and wept again' while writing it.

A CHRISTMAS CAROL
PUBLISHED 1843

A Christmas Carol is the tale of Ebenezer Scrooge who, as a boy, had been kind and warm-hearted. But life has turned him into a miserly skinflint, living alone. He is visited by three spirits.

The Spirit of Christmas Past takes him to look again at his childish self. The Spirit of Christmas Present appears to Scrooge in the form of a bare-chested Bacchus. This is not Father Christmas as we know him, but as Dickens described him the two characters are undoubtedly related.

It was clothed in one simple green robe or mantle, bordered with white fur.

This garment hung so loosely on the figure that its capacious breast was bare . . . its feet . . . were also bare . . . and on its head it wore no other covering than a holly wreath set here and there with shining icicles.

The spirit awakens emotions long since dead in Scrooge, by taking him to see the poverty and suffering of his clerk Bob Cratchit's family, caring in squalor for their crippled child Tiny Tim.

The Spirit of Christmas Yet to Come invites Scrooge to observe how the world reacts to his death. He watches as the bedclothes are torn from beneath his corpse, while it still lies on the bed and how colleagues do not care about his demise. Image after image breaks him down until he awakens, in terror, to discover it was all a dream.

From that time forward he determines to make Christmas special for everyone around him.

It was Prince Albert himself who introduced the first Christmas tree to the Royal circle and encouraging the giving of presents, which he said was 'a very pretty idea.'

Dickens had expended his usual energy into the writing of *A Christmas Carol* – which was the first book that appeared complete and not in instalments and was also the subject of his first public reading.

When it was finished he 'broke out like a Madman' with a whole succession of Christmas parties at his London house in Devonshire Terrace.

'Such dancings, such conjurings, such blind man's buffings, such theatre goings, such kissings-out of old years and kissings-in of new ones never took place in these parts before.'

Dickens reciting a favourite passage. From a Harry Furniss sketch.
Photo: Dickens House Museum, London.

Over Christmas 1843, Dickens' friend Jane Welsh Carlisle was invited to help out at a birthday party for the actor Henry Macready's young daughter Nina. Dickens was there as conjuror/magician and children's entertainer.

The party was a huge success and, according to Jane Carlise later became 'like the rape of the Sabines' with everyone dancing and whirling all evening.

But his promotion of Christmas as a time of goodwill was, for him, more than a time of revelry. From 1843 Dickens also began to immerse himself more and more in children's welfare. The seven children of an actor friend, Edward Elton, were orphaned when their father was drowned off Holy Island. Dickens formed a committee to care for the family, raised money and arranged apprenticeships. His work brought him into contact with the great social reformer Baroness Angela Burdett Coutts – who later paid for his son, Charley, to go to Eton.

In 1844 came *The Chimes*, a bitter attack on the Poor Law and its assumption that the poor were born bad. Dickens explained: 'My purpose was, in a whimsical kind of masque, which the good humour of the season justified, to awaken some forgiving and forbearing thoughts never out of season in a Christian land.'

In 1845 *The Cricket on the Hearth* appeared and was hugely sucessful. This concerns a toymaker called Caleb.

There were Noah's Arks, in which the Birds and Beasts were an uncommonly tight fit. There were scores of melancholy little carts which . . . performed most doleful music. Many small fiddles, drums, and other instruments of torture; no end of cannon, shields, swords, spears and guns . . . Caleb and his daughter sat at work. The Blind Girl busy as a Doll's dressmaker; and Caleb painting and glazing. . .

THE CHRISTMAS STORIES

There is probably a smell of roasted chestnuts and other good comfortable things all the time, for we are telling Winter stories – Ghost stories, or more shame for us – round the Christmas fire. . .

EVERY year between 1850 and 1867 Dickens wrote a Christmas Story for *Household Words* and for *All the Year Round*. They cast a cosy, some-

Carols by candlelight outside the cathedral.
Photo: Rochester Upon Medway City Council.

readings, recitals, music hall and ghost tours, toffee apples, muffins and the Seven Poor Travellers Procession. It all comes to an end on the Sunday night with a torchlight procession and carols outside the Cathedral.

It was always Dickens' dream that Christmas could be made to last all the year round. 'That way,' he said, 'the world would be made a better place.'

BIBLIOGRAPHY

A Week's Tramp in Dickens Land by William R Hughes. Chapman and Hall 1891.

Charles Dickens by G K Chesterton. Methuen 1906.

Charles Dickens' Childhood by Michael Allen. MacMillan 1988.

Charles Dickens and Rochester by Robert Langton. Chapman and Hall 1880.

Charles Dickens as I knew him by George Dolby. T Fisher Unwin 1885.

Charles Dickens by Alan Watts. Studio Editions of London 1991.

Dickens at Gad's Hill by Alan Watts. Elvenden Press, 1989.

Dickens by Peter Ackroyd. Sinclair Stevenson 1990.

Dickens and Daughter by Gladys Storey. Frederick Muller 1939.

Dickens Centenary Week. Dickens Fellowship 1912.

Dickens Festival Pageant programme 1951.

Dickens of London by Wolf Mankowitz. Weidenfeld and Nicolson 1976.

The Decline of English Murder and Other Essays by George Orwell. Penguin 1965 (first edition 1940).

Illustrated Guide to Dickensian Rochester by Edwin Harris. Edwin Harris 1920.

The Charles Dickens Companion by Michael and Mollie Hardwick. Osprey 1973.

The Charles Dickens Show by Raymund Fitzsimmon. Geoffrey Bles 1970.

The Childhood and Youth of Charles Dickens by Robert Langton. Hutchinson 1912.

The Dickens Country by F G Kitton. Black 1905.

The Dickensian published monthly by the Dickens Fellowship.

The Life of Charles Dickens by John Forster. Chapman and Hall 1872.